PRESIDENTIAL
FOREIGN LANGUAGE

TRIVIA
SECOND EDITION

GREGORY J. NEDVED

Copyright © 2024 Greg Nedved

ISBN (Paperback): 979-8-89381-108-7
ISBN (eBook): 979-8-89381-107-0
ISBN (Hardback): 979-8-89381-109-4

All rights reserved. No part of this book may be reproduced or transmitted in any form or by any means, electronic or mechanical, including photocopying, recording, or by any information storage and retrieval system, without permission in writing from the copyright owner. The views expressed in this work are solely those of the author and do not necessarily reflect the views of the publisher, and the publisher hereby disclaims any responsibility for them.

508 West 26th Street KEARNEY, NE 68848
402-819-3224
info@medialiteraryexcellence.com

TABLE OF CONTENTS

True Or False 1

Future Presidents 9

Presidents In Office 25

Ex-Presidents 37

Presidents General 40

English Is A Language Too 49

Thomas Jefferson 58

TRUE OR FALSE

1. James Garfield said, "No instance exists of a person writing two languages perfectly."

    ✓ False (Thomas Jefferson in a 1785 letter to J. Bannister)

2. Germany decided that a Franklin Delano Roosevelt-Winston Churchill wartime meeting would be at the White House since white is "blanca," and house is "casa" in Spanish.

    ✓ True—although this story is unverified; the White House location was determined by German analysis of decrypted messages; the actual meeting was in January 1943 in Casablanca, Morocco.

3. Gerald Ford was annoyed with his interpreter for waiting too long to ask him what he wanted for dessert during a visit to Vienna, Austria.

    ✓ False (it was Jimmy Carter on June 15, 1979, who finally responded with a scowl, "I made my selection a long time ago."). The interpreter blamed the incident on Carter's jet lag.

4. James Madison said that "English is destined to be in the next and succeeding centuries, more generally the language of the world than Latin was in the last or French is in the present age."

- ✓ False (it was John Adams in 1780; he knew both Latin and French).

5. Ulysses Grant remained in Mexico for several months after the Mexican-American War, learning Spanish.

    - ✓ True (also exploring Mexico)

6. The Unkechaug tribe of Long Island, New York, used James Monroe's vocabulary list to restore its lost language.

    - ✓ False (Thomas Jefferson compiled the list during a 1791 visit to the tribe).

7. Thomas Jefferson considered language to be a science.

    - ✓ False ("I do not pretend that language is science. It is only an instrument for the attainment of science.") (1782 Notes on the State of Virginia)

8. Abraham Lincoln received telegraph messages in Russian from General John C. Frémont in the Civil War.

    - ✓ False (it was Hungarian; Lincoln's translator was Albert de Zeyk, who manned the telegraph office in Washington).

9. Theodore Roosevelt had "Qui plantavit curabit" (He who planted will preserve) as a family motto.

- ✓ True (so did Franklin Delano Roosevelt)

10. The first book that Millard Fillmore ever purchased was a Bible.

    - ✓ False (it was a dictionary, which he read diligently while running a carding machine as a youth).

11. Theodore Roosevelt was an avid collector of Native American vocabulary.

    - ✓ False (it was Thomas Jefferson he believed it was possible to trace the origins of Native Americans by examining their language roots).

12. Spanish was not one of diplomat James Buchanan's languages.

    - ✓ True (He knew some French and probably a little Russian).

13. There is no Latin inscribed on the Washington Monument.

    - ✓ False ("laus Deo" (praise be to God) is inscribed on the east side at the peak).

14. James Madison was able to translate the Latin orations of Grotius, Pufendorf, and Vattel.

- ✓ True (he also studied Horace and Ovid).

15. James Monroe translated into English the German language works of Friedrich Gentz and Christoph Martin Wieland.

    - ✓ False (it was John Quincy Adams, who tackled German while a diplomat in Berlin, 1797-1801).

16. A Mexican officer during the Mexican-American War tried to negotiate with Zachary Taylor in French.

    - ✓ True (he tried French after Spanish failed).

17. George Washington did not have a translator when he signed a French document at Fort Necessity in 1754 admitting responsibility for the death of a French diplomat.

    - ✓ False: His translator was Jacob Van Braam. After winning the Battle of Fort Necessity, the French forced Washington to sign the document.

18. Ronald Reagan, in his June 12, 1987, speech, said "Lass' sie nach Berlin kommen" (Let them come to Berlin).

    - ✓ False (it was John Kennedy in a June 26, 1963 speech).

19. Jimmy Carter had a Russian interpreter whose father had been a Soviet spy in the United States.
    - ✓ False (it was Richard Nixon and the interpreter's name was Victor Sukhodrev).

20. Van Buren translates to "of or from Buren."
    - ✓ True (Martin Van Buren visited Buren, Holland, in 1853)

21. Bill Clinton once gave up trying to convert money at a foreign airport because he couldn't communicate with the person handling the transaction.
    - ✓ False (it was George H.W. Bush, head of the US Liaison Office in China, 1974-1975).

22. George Washington thought French was the international language of polite society.
    - ✓ True (he thought it was the most practical foreign language).

23. Gerald Ford's high school Latin teacher was Amanda Ardelia Palmer.
    - ✓ False (she taught Harry Truman for two years).

24. Lyndon Johnson never took any foreign language classes in college.

- ✓ True (he did take high school German though).

25. Franklin Delano Roosevelt, in an 1896 letter to his parents, once signed his name in Greek.

    - ✓ True (he was then a student at Groton).

26. Herbert Hoover thought his Chinese was better than his wife's.

    - ✓ False (he thought she was especially good at reading it) (she actually knew several languages).

27. Monsieur Partout, James Monroe's informal French language instructor, was also Thomas Jefferson's chef.

    - ✓ True (Partout stayed behind when Jefferson went to France)

28. Every president since George Walker Bush has had Spanish language content on the White House website.

    - ✓ False (despite promises, it never happened under Donald Trump).

29. Woodrow Wilson did not support the usage of English as the official language at the Versailles Peace Conference ending World War I.

    ✓ False (in the end, both French and English were the official languages).

30. Japanese Prime Minister Yoshirō Mori meant to say, "How are you?" in English but instead said, "Who are you?" when he first met Barack Obama.

    ✓ False (the story is popular, but Mori and Obama apparently never met).

31. Woodrow Wilson refused to defend a German language instructor fired because he opposed US entry into WWI.

    ✓ False (he wrote a letter of support for the professor).

32. The interpreters had a hard time keeping up when Theodore Roosevelt got into a shouting match with a Spanish colonel.

    ✓ False (it was Andrew Jackson, who was replacing the man as governor of Florida, August 1821).

33. Thomas Jefferson once wrote that the oldest American history was written chiefly in Spanish.

- ✓ True (he still thought French was more important though).

34. Zachary Taylor instructed his French chef to translate for an unexpected White House visitor.

    - ✓ False (it was Andrew Jackson; the Portuguese Minister showed up at the White House by mistake; Jackson first asked his porter, Jimmy O'Neill, to try him in Irish!)

FUTURE PRESIDENTS

1. Who used "United States language" in a sentence?

    ✓ Harry Truman on April 17, 1918 (he wrote "...and everything was in good United States language").

2. June Steck taught Latin in high school to which president?

    ✓ Richard Nixon (she taught him Virgil's Aeneid; he played Aeneas in a school play)

3. Zenas Caldwell helped whom master Latin?

    ✓ Franklin Pierce (he gave a graduation speech in Latin from Bowdoin College but was bad in the language before Caldwell became his roommate)

4. To get into what university, John Adams translated a passage from English into Latin, requiring vocabulary he did not know?

    ✓ Harvard (he was allowed a dictionary and was given plenty of time to complete the test).

5. Where did Baptist Harry Truman attend a French-language Catholic mass?

- ✓ In France as a soldier in World War I (he could not understand a word)

6. What language did Rutherford Hayes spend a lot of time studying as a law student?

    - ✓ German (at Columbus, Ohio, and Harvard University; also some French at Harvard)

7. Who once recorded the scientfic Latin names for a salamander, mouse, eagle, wolf, and bear in his diary?

    - ✓ Theodore Roosevelt (as a boy—some of his names were wrong)

8. Who paid for German lessons so that he could read the works of Friedrich Schiller within three years?

    - ✓ Rutherford Hayes (as a lawyer in training at Columbus, Ohio)

9. Who needed extra tutoring to pass the Latin entrance exam for the Choate School?

    - ✓ John Kennedy (he went to high school there, 1931–1935).

10. Who hit his interpreter with a hammer?

    - ✓ Herbert Hoover (as an engineer in China, he was once in a flooded mineshaft and threw the hammer to alert his interpreter, who ran away and reported Hoover killed!)

11. Who is affiliated with the Latin inscription "Ici. Toed. Foet" (icy toad feet)?

    ✓ Harry Truman (he remembered seeing it written on an apothecary jar in a drugstore he once worked in)

12. Who said the following, "Yo quiero construir puentes, no paredes" (I want to build bridges, not walls)?

    ✓ George W. Bush (2000 presidential election campaign)

13. Who opined that "You will learn to speak it [French] better from women and children in three months, than from men in a year?"

    ✓ Thomas Jefferson (1787 letter to T. M. Randolph Jr.)

14. Who said: "The Great Spirit would have made all tribes speak one language if they were to be one nation?"

    ✓ William Henry Harrison reminded Shawnee Chief Tecumseh that he did not speak for all tribes, August 1810.

15. Joseph Marsh was the Latin tutor for which president?

    ✓ John Adams (thanks to him, Adams passed his Harvard Latin entrance exam)

16. Who opined that Greek and Latin were not dead languages?

    ✓ Calvin Coolidge (address at University of Pennsylvania, July 7, 1921)

17. When John C. Fremont sent orders to Ulysses Grant to capture Paducah, Kentucky, in 1861, what language were the orders in?

    ✓ Hungarian (Frémont, Grant's Civil War commander, had Hungarian officers under him and liked using their language for sensitive communiqués)

18. Who found humorous a wartime German-English-German translation mishap?

    ✓ George Washington (commands to soldiers from Baron von Steuben translated into English went back into German—von Steuben did not realize at first that these soldiers were actually German)

19. Who was identified with "De Triumphis Romanourium" (The Triumphant Roman)?

- ✓ Franklin Pierce performed this as part of his junior class Latin project at Bowdoin College in Maine.

20. Who "did well enough in Latin and Greek, but his taste ran toward government, law, and oratory"?

    - ✓ Benjamin Harrison (the source was Chicago preacher David Swing, Harrison's fraternity brother at Miami University of Ohio).

21. Who had the following foreign language academic record: High School Latin Club; College French grades of B, D, and C?

    - ✓ Gerald Ford (he went to college at the University of Michigan).

22. Who wrote the following: "I have so far mastered the French language.... It will be some time, however, before I shall speak it fluently."?

    - ✓ James Buchanan (in 1832, while serving as minister to Russia)

23. What language did Woodrow Wilson learn to earn his doctorate from Johns Hopkins University?

    - ✓ German (he never claimed any proficiency in it though).

24. Who offered to play the piano after his high school Latin play ended?

    ✓ Richard Nixon (he offered to do this after the play got only lukewarm applause because "I'll do anything to make the party a success")

25. How many semesters at Whittier College did Richard Nixon take French?

    ✓ Seven (he felt confident enough to add French phrases when taking notes in later years)

26. Who said the following about German emigrants in Pennsylvania: "They would never speak English, but when spoken to, they speak all Dutch?".

    ✓ George Washington (his 1748 diary, based on an encounter with them (probably the Pennsylvania Dutch) in a surveying trip to the Shenandoah Valley)

27. According to James Madison, he spoke French with what kind of an accent?

    ✓ Scotch (Madison entered Princeton already knowing a little French but stood out with his accent)

28. Who had a nickname that is a foreign language?

- ✓ Ronald Reagan (he was called Dutch in his youth by his father because he looked like a "fat little Dutchman" and had a "Dutch boy" haircut)

29. Who bought foreign language printing materials to win an election?

    - ✓ Abraham Lincoln (in 1859, he purchased the printing press and language type of a German-language Illinois newspaper to win the state's German vote in the 1860 presidential election)

30. Dr. FW Day taught Old Testament Hebrew to which president?

    - ✓ William McKinley (in Poland, Ohio; Day was a Methodist Episcopal minister there)

31. Who helped translate a medieval work into English from Latin?

    - ✓ Herbert Hoover (he and wife, Lou, in 1912 translated the 1556 mining classic "De Re Metallica").

32. Elizabeth Buck was which president's Latin teacher?

    - ✓ Bill Clinton (he had to memorize lots of lines from Caesar's "Gallic Wars")

33. Donald Robertson taught Greek, Latin and French to which future president?

    ✓ James Madison (Madison later acknowledged that "all that [he has] been in life [he owes] largely to that man."

34. Who studied Hebrew at the College of New Jersey (now Princeton University)?

    ✓ James Madison (he spent an extra year there to master it)

35. Who did the German-language press support in the 1920 presidential election?

    ✓ Warren Harding ("A vote for Harding is a vote against the persecutions suffered by German Americans during the war (World War 1)").

36. Which president lived with a German family for a year as a youth?

    ✓ Theodore Roosevelt (even so, speaking German was hard for him; he read it well)

37. Who provided financial support for a German-language newspaper to win an election?

- ✓ Millard Fillmore (Buffalo, NY newspaper in 1843; as a Whig, he lost the New York governor's race in 1844)

38. Who thought the French film "Femmes des France" (Women of France) had the wrong title?

    - ✓ Harry Truman (he saw it in 1918 in France but thought the film had nothing to do with the title)

39. Which president delayed a response to a letter because he did not trust his French?

    - ✓ William Henry Harrison (he did not completely understand the French used in the 1804 letter by the author, fur trader August Choteau).

40. Which president thought that the French comedies were the best way to learn French?

    - ✓ John Adams (1779 diary entry—"The language is nowhere better spoken than at the Comédie").

41. Which president was humorously discouraged from giving speeches in Latin?

    - ✓ Warren Harding (steel magnate Charles Schwab advised Harding against this at the 1919 Pennsylvania Society annual dinner, which both attended)

42. Who received a congratulatory note saying "Vive la République" (Long Live the Republic) after winning an election?

    ✓ James Monroe (In 1799 he received this note containing this French phrase after winning the Virginia governor's race)

43. Who once defended Catiline (accused of conspiring against the Roman Republic) in a high school Latin-language mock trial?

    ✓ Bill Clinton (this experience supposedly convinced him to study law)

44. Which president heard shouts of "Vive les États-Unis" (Long live the United States) when he spoke to the French national legislature?

    ✓ James Monroe (on August 15, 1794, as the US minister to France)

45. Who said, "When you meet my wife, will you please tell her to stop laughing at me when I take my Chinese lesson?".

    ✓ George H.W. Bush (his comments on his first day of Chinese lessons as U.S. liaison to China, 1974-1975)

46. Lyndon Baines Johnson used banners in which language to greet visitors to his Texas ranch in 1961 and 1963?

    ✓ German (Konrad Adenauer, 1961; Ludwig Erhard, 1963—both leaders of West Germany)

47. According to John Adams, who spoke French poorly and understood considerably less French than he let on?

    ✓ His fellow diplomat in Paris, representing the new United States, Benjamin Franklin.

48. What language did the Iranian ambassador use during a March 1975 meeting in China with George H. W. Bush?

    ✓ French (Bush's French was not as good as the Ambassador's English).

49. Which president toured Prague, Czechoslovakia, using German?

    ✓ Bill Clinton (1968; his tour guide knew no English)

50. Which president studied German because he was "impressed by the clarity and precision of the language" and because he was interested in Germany?"

- ✓ Bill Clinton (he studied it at Georgetown University)

51. Which president cited the French expression "C'est la guerre" (It's the war) to rationalize the death of an acquaintance?

    - ✓ Harry Truman (reference to the WWI death of his acquaintance, Rufe Montyall)

52. Where was Richard Nixon when unfriendly signs showed up at one of his political rallies?

    - ✓ Chinatown in Los Angeles in 1962 (the unfriendly signs were written in Chinese). One said, "What about the huge loan?" (a reference to his connections to Howard Hughes)

53. Who used the phrase "Fiat justitia, pereat coelum" (Let justice be done though heaven perish) in a letter to his father?

    - ✓ John Quincy Adams (to his father John Adams) in 1816

54. Who learned German, French and Latin from Jeanne Sandoz?

    - ✓ Franklin Delano Roosevelt (she was his Swiss governess growing up)

55. Who "had the great pleasure of failing the most outrageous Greek exam that has ever been known in the history of education?"

    ✓ Franklin Delano Roosevelt (a student at Groton; he wrote this to his mother in 1897)

56. Which president was the Latin salutatorian of his graduating college class?

    ✓ James Polk (he gave the welcoming address at his graduation ceremony at the University of North Carolina in 1818 in Latin)

57. Which president negotiated with a priest in Spanish for use of a church?

    ✓ Ulysses Grant (during the Mexican-American War, he persuaded a Mexican priest to let US forces mount howitzers in the church's belfry)

58. Who translated German with his wife at home rather than go to Germany alone?

    ✓ Woodrow Wilson (he wanted to go to Berlin to work on a textbook but passed since he could not afford to take his family with him)

59. Who married his foreign language student?

- ✓ James Garfield (Lucretia Rudolph, his former Greek language student at the Western Reserve Eclectic Institute (later Hiram College) in Ohio)

60. Who said, "All I can say [in French] is "je ne comprend pas" [I do not understand], and I'm not sure of that?"

    - ✓ Harry Truman (in a 1918 letter to his wife)

61. Who regretted saying "Porque? Tenemos bastante tiempo. Why hurry"? (Why? We have enough time. Why hurry?) to Filipino guests during a social call?

    - ✓ Governor-General William Howard Taft of the Philippines (he actually wanted his guests to leave but was trying to be polite—they stayed another hour).

62. From whom might you have heard "alles willkommen" (all welcome) on the campaign trail?

    - ✓ James Garfield (he often spoke in German with German Americans he encountered while out campaigning).

63. In "The China Diary of George H. W. Bush: The Making of a Global President," Bush provided the Chinese name for what sport?

    - ✓ Tennis ("da wangqiu"—to play tennis)

64. Who said the following: "I don't speak a foreign language. It's embarrassing!"

    ✓ Barack Obama (town hall meeting in Dayton, Ohio, on July 11, 2008)

65. Who used a Hindi expression on the presidential campaign trial?

    ✓ Donald Trump (in 2016; "Ab ki baar Trump sarka") ("This time Trump government").

66. Who used the Arabic expression "Inshallah" on occasion during his presidential campaign?

    ✓ Joe Biden (in 2020; it means "God knows" but can also be used to express skepticism)

67. Who received translation assistance from Louis-Guillaume Otto?

    ✓ James Monroe (he translated Monroe's 1794 speech to the French Convention into French)

68. Who helped Rutherford Hayes improve his Greek and Latin and taught him French?

    ✓ His older sister Fanny (he was a teenager)

69. Why didn't Harry Truman learn French while stationed in France during WWI?

- He had "too much artillery to learn" (this is what he told his wife, Bess)

PRESIDENTS IN OFFICE

1. Which president is connected to the "jelly doughnut" mistranslation story?

    ✓ John Kennedy. The "Ich bin ein Berliner" (I am a Berliner) line from his June 26, 1963, speech has been famously mistranslated as "I am a jelly doughnut."

2. Who had to take a membership oath in Sioux to join the Singing Tribe of Wahoo?

    ✓ Dwight Eisenhower (in 1953; The Singing Tribe of Wahoo were Black Hills (South Dakota) boosters)

3. Which country did Bill Clinton inadvertently insult by placing his interpreter between himself and the country's leader?

    ✓ South Korea (in Seoul on July 10, 1993; South Korean president was Kim Young-san)

4. Franklin Delano Roosevelt was upset when told his French was "as good" as whose?

    ✓ Winston Churchill (Roosevelt felt his accent was not only "infinitely superior, but his French profanity is so explosive that you had better not be within a half mile of him when it goes off."

5. Who confronted his vice president with the Caesarian "Et tu Brute"? (and you, Brutus)?

    ✓ Andrew Jackson (May 30, 1830, after he learned that Vice President John C. Calhoun did not support his 1818 military incursion into Spanish Florida.)

6. Which president said the following: "My French and German are terrible?"

    ✓ Barack Obama (a town meeting at Strasbourg, France, on April 3, 2009).

7. "When I left the United States this morning" was mistranslated as "When I abandoned the United States." Who was the misquoted president?

    ✓ Jimmy Carter (the language was Polish; a December 29, 1977 speech)

8. Which president corrected the Latin of a Supreme Chief Justice?

    ✓ Harry Truman correctly told Fred Vinson that the Latin for "Carthage ought to be destroyed" was "Delenda est Carthago." Vinson said it was "Carthago delenda est".

9. Who said the following: "At the outset, I regret that I find it necessary to have a translator. I do say, though,

that having heard his translation, he had every word right—every word?"

- ✓ Richard Nixon (his address to the German parliament (Bundestag) on February 26, 1969)

10. When Joe James sent a letter congratulating Grover Cleveland on his 1886 marriage to Frances Folsom, he signed it in which two languages?

    - ✓ English and Chinese (James, who was Chinese, also sent the letter to thank Cleveland for his treatment of Chinese living within the United States).

11. Which world leader said the following after being asked about Bill Clinton's impending impeachment: "Excuse me, I'm a little bit tired. I prefer to speak in my language".

    - ✓ Czech president Václav Havel (September 16, 1998, Clinton-Havel press conference in Washington). Havel then said in Czech that this was an American issue, not affecting him.

12. Which president said the following: "I come here today because wherever I go, whatever I do: 'ich hab noch einen Koffer' in Berlin" (I still have a suitcase in Berlin)?

✓ Ronald Reagan (June 12, 1987, at the Brandenburg Gate in West Berlin to commemorate Berlin's 750th birthday)

13. Which president ended a press conference in Portugal with the following: "So obrigado (thank you). Thank you very much?"

    ✓ Barack Obama (NATO Summit in Lisbon on November 20, 2010)

14. Which president ended a speech with "Thank you for giving me a chance to come by to visit with you. 'Que Dios los endiga.' (May God bless you.) Thank you all?"

    ✓ George W. Bush (April 20, 2005; US Hispanic Chamber of Commerce conference in Washington)

15. Who chose the hymn "Eine Feste Burg Ist Unser Gott" (A Mighty Fortress Is Our God) for the German-language service he attended on Palm Sunday?

    ✓ Theodore Roosevelt (he attended the morning all-German service at the German Congregational Church in Sioux Falls, South Dakota, April 5, 1903)

16. Thamsanqa Jantjie did a fake signing for which president?

- ✓ Barack Obama (Nelson Mandela's South Africa funeral, December 10, 2013; sign language experts called Thamsanqa Jantjie a fake)

17. Who said the following: "Mr. Interpreter, you are blocking my view of the Jefferson Memorial!"?

    - ✓ Lyndon Johnson (he and the interpreter, Harry Obst, were waiting for a German visitor to arrive. Despite this incident, Obst thought Johnson treated interpreters well).

18. Who received a thank-you note written in Hawaiian (along with an English translation)?

    - ✓ Abraham Lincoln (he sent Missionary James Kekela gifts for saving a US sailor from Marquesas island cannibals. Kekela's thank you letter arrived after Lincoln's assassination.)

19. What language did James Polk use when a Peruvian diplomat in December 1846 presented himself formally in French?

    - ✓ English (he did not know French, the language of diplomats, nor Spanish, the diplomat's native language).

20. The phrase "sic semper tyrannis" (thus, death always to tyrants) was scribbled on the campaign biography of which president?

    ✓ John Tyler (full scribble was "A Traitor to the Whig Party, Sic Semper Tyrannis;" his 1844 campaign biography was called "Life of John Tyler").

21. Who mentioned English, Spanish, Portuguese, and French in an annual message?

    ✓ William McKinley (on December 5, 1898, he mentioned the four languages of the Bureau of the American Republics)

22. How many times did John Kennedy say "Ich bin ein Berliner" (I am a Berliner) in his famous 26 June 1963 speech?

    ✓ Twice (at the beginning and the end); He also said "Civis romanus sum" (I am a citizen of Rome).

23. What president adopted the Latin motto "suaviter in modo, fortiter in re" (gently in manner, firmly in action) to show that he was brainy?

    ✓ Dwight Eisenhower (When he became president, he put this motto on his desk and told a reporter, "That proves I'm an egghead.")

24. What president used the Latin expression "Ex necessitate rei" (from the necessity of the thing) in a letter to a Catholic organization?

    ✓ Grover Cleveland (January 26, 1887 letter to the Committee of the Catholic Club of Philadelphia, turning down an invitation to a banquet for Cardinal James Gibbons)

25. Which president mentioned a foreign language Bible in a special message to Congress?

    ✓ Chester Arthur (on February 3, 1885, he requested that Congress transfer to the US government a Coptic (Egyptian) Bible belonging to the dying Ulysses Grant?

26. Which president used the Latin phrase "In hoc signo vinces" (In this sign, you will conquer) in his presidential campaign?

    ✓ Benjamin Harrison (unsuccessful 1892 reelection campaign; used on campaign paraphernalia e.g., paperweights, studs, noisemakers)

27. A December 29, 1977 speech by Jimmy Carter is well known for its humorous mistranslations. What was the culprit language?

- ✓ Polish (for example, "I have come to learn your opinions and understand your desires for the future" was translated as "I desire the Poles carnally.")

28. Who was the first president to openly use Latin in a presidential campaign?

    - ✓ Benjamin Harrison (his unsuccessful 1892 reelection campaign)

29. Which president used the Latin "terra incognita" (unknown land) in a Minnesota speech?

    - ✓ William McKinley (October 12, 1899, Minneapolis—reference to purchase of Alaska in 1867)

30. Which president made the following statement in Berlin: "Was immer sei, Berlin bleibt frei" (No matter what may be, Berlin will stay free)?

    - ✓ Jimmy Carter (end of his July 15, 1978, Berlin speech).

31. Who acknowledged that he was "not the best spokesman in the Russian language?"

    - ✓ Gerald Ford: In 1974, he asked Soviet Ambassador Anatoly Dobrynin to help him pronounce the names of two cosmonauts, members of the July 1975 Apollo-Soyuz space team.

32. George H.W. Bush's vomiting mishap created a special word in which language?

    ✓ Japanese (Bushu-suru—"to do the Bush thing'). Bush threw up on the Japanese Prime Minister at a 1992 state dinner in Japan.

33. Who rejected the ambassadorship nomination of William F. McCombs because he did not speak the language of the host nation?

    ✓ Woodrow Wilson (McCombs did not know Spanish, making him unqualified to be US Ambassador to Mexico)

34. Who said the following: "They were starting to learn German in Paris before the U.S. came along?"

    ✓ Donald Trump (November 13, 2018, tweet comment on French national defense strategy)

35. Who, at the recommendation of his German interpreter (Harry Obst), agreed to lengthen his text before pausing for the German translation?

    ✓ Ronald Reagan (1982 Berlin speech, which was well received)

36. Who said the following: "Amerika steht an ihrer Seite jetzt und für immer" (America stands on your side now and forever)?

    ✓ Bill Clinton (July 12, 1994, at Berlin's Brandenburg Gate)

37. Which language did Herbert Hoover and his wife, Lou Henry, speak in the White House to ensure complete privacy?

    ✓ Chinese-Mandarin (he thought that she was better in the language because the Chinese always spoke to her in Chinese but English to him!)

38. Which president was sworn in on a Bible written in a modern foreign language?

    ✓ Franklin Delano Roosevelt (he used an old family Bible written in Dutch for all four of his presidential inaugurations).

39. What language did Donald Trump predict Americans would have to learn if he was defeated for reelection in 2020?

    ✓ Chinese (August 11, 2020 interview)

40. Who was the first president to visit Gallaudet University (a school for the deaf in Washington, DC)?

- ✓ Ulysses Grant (school's first commencement ceremony in 1869)

41. Who created Gallaudet University?

    - ✓ Abraham Lincoln (signed its charter bill into law in 1864)

42. How many years of French did Joe Biden take in high school and college?

    - ✓ Five (what he told Canadian Prime Minister Justin Trudeau, February 23, 2021)

43. Who thought it was "ridiculous and childish" to prohibit instruction of what foreign language?

    - ✓ Woodrow Wilson, German (the United States was fighting Germany in WWI at the time).

44. Who was given the Native American name Wamblee-Tokaha, "Leading Eagle?"

    - ✓ Calvin Coolidge (his given name for induction into the Sioux tribe in 1927)

45. Who had Paul Mantoux as his French interpreter?

    - ✓ Woodrow Wilson (at the 1919 Versailles Conference)

46. Who wrote a letter supporting a fired foreign language college instructor even though the instructor was critical of his policies?

    ✓ Woodrow Wilson (the German professor, from Goucher College in Maryland, did not embrace US involvement in WWI)

47. According to Joe Biden, what percentage of US **schoolchildren** can speak Spanish?

    ✓ 25% (Cinco de Mayo White House event speech, May 5, 2022)

48. Who had his degree citation read to him in Latin?

    ✓ Bill Clinton (Oxford University doctorate, June 8, 1994)

49. Who mistakenly thought that Austrian was a language?

    ✓ Barack Obama (NATO conference, April 6, 2009)

50. How many languages did Joe Biden speak in a video shown at an Air Force workshop on August 26, 2022?

    ✓ Five—but this never happened (he was shown speaking them at a UN conference, an example of "deepfake" technology).

EX-PRESIDENTS

1. Who gave a copy of the Lord's Prayer in Anglo-Saxon to a colleague?

    ✓ Thomas Jefferson (1825 letter to J. Evelyn Denison)

2. Which prominent Native American leader's untranslated speech actually insulted Ulysses Grant, who was in the audience?

    ✓ Sitting Bull (a September 8, 1883, ceremony commemorating the completion of the Northern Pacific Railroad)

3. Who wrote the following Latin expression in his diary two days before his death: "Non nobis, Domine, non nobis, sed nomini tuo do gloriam"?

    ✓ John Quincy Adams ("Not to us, O Lord, not to us, but to thy name give glory," written on February 21, 1848)

4. Who said' "The birds were not speaking English, and I knew enough Russian to know they weren't speaking Russian? As it turned out, they spoke only Malaysian?"

    ✓ Richard Nixon (two parrots were loudly squawking while he was visiting Russian General Aleksandr V. Rutskoi in March 1994).

5. Who once asked in Spanish, "Are you honest, or are you thieves?" (Estan ustedes honestos o ladrones?)?

    ✓ Jimmy Carter (as an elections supervisor in Panama, he confronted judges rigging an election for Manuel Noriega)

6. Who said the following: "No man should accept a degree he cannot read?"

    ✓ Millard Fillmore (he turned down an honorary doctorate in 1855 from Oxford because he could not understand the Latin written on the diploma)

7. Which country did Jimmy Carter criticize in a Spanish-language television and radio speech on May 14, 2002?

    ✓ Cuba (the speech was actually at Havana University, with Cuban leader, Fidel Castro in attendance).

8. Who is identified with the phrase "Adieu—'sic iter ad astra" (Goodbye—such is the way to the stars or immortality)?

    ✓ Andrew Johnson (he used it, believing he was about to die—he lived two more years!)

9. Who was identified with the Yu Cong Eng v. Trinidad court case that allowed business records to be kept in Chinese?

    ✓ William Howard Taft (the case involved the Philippines; he made his 1926 ruling as the Chief Justice of the Supreme Court)

10. What event so shook John Quincy Adams that he could only murmur "Dies Irae" (Wrath of God)?

    ✓ An 1844 explosion on the USS Princeton that killed two of John Tyler's cabinet members

11. Who made two public addresses in the West Indies in French?

    ✓ Theodore Roosevelt in 1916 (supposedly he spoke French with a German accent)

12. Who studied French on the Portuguese island of Madeira?

    ✓ Franklin Pierce (and his wife) in 1858.

PRESIDENTS GENERAL

1. Which president's motto was "exitus acta probat" (the outcome is the test of the act)?

    ✓ George Washington (taken from the family coat of arms),

2. How many foreign languages did John Quincy Adams know?

    ✓ Six (Latin, Greek, Dutch, Italian, German, French) (maybe Russian too)

3. Who supposedly used sign language when having a private conversation with his family?

    ✓ Calvin Coolidge (his wife, Grace, taught deaf students)

4. Which languages were John Adams "too old" to learn?

    ✓ Chinese and "the Semitic tongues" (he wanted to read the ancient texts)

5. Who routinely reads the Bible in different languages?

    ✓ John Quincy Adams (in English, French, and German)

6. Which presidential combination documented Delaware Indian words?

- ✓ Thomas Jefferson and James Madison: Jefferson collected eighty words of the Minsi dialect (Delaware); Madison recorded 267 words of the Southern Unami dialect (New Jersey)

7. "No quiero destruir un idioma muy bonito" (I don't want to destroy a beautiful language) is a favorite phrase of which president?

    - ✓ George W. Bush, who actually had some proficiency in Spanish

8. What two sign language letters does Abraham Lincoln supposedly spell out with his hands at the Lincoln Memorial?

    - ✓ A (left hand) and L (right hand) (for Abraham Lincoln) (the National Park Service disputes that he spells out these letters)

9. Which president preferred to read Roman military history, e.g., Julius Caesar, in Latin?

    - ✓ William Henry Harrison (he learned his Latin at Hampden-Sydney College in Virginia, where he also learned French)

10. Maryland Congressman William Vans Murray helped which president with language preservation?

✓ Thomas Jefferson (Murray collected Nanticoke (an Algonquian language) vocabulary words at his request)

11. Which two presidents were fond of this quote: "In the Chinese language, the word 'crisis' is composed of two characters, one representing danger and the other, opportunity?"

    ✓ John Kennedy and Richard Nixon ("Crisis" in Chinese is Weiji. Although Wei means "danger," Ji does not necessarily mean "opportunity")

12. Chester Arthur felt comfortable enough to converse in what foreign languages?

    ✓ Greek and Latin (his father, William Arthur, a Baptist minister, supervised his training).

13. Who claimed that he could find nobody in Duysberg, Germany, who could understand him?

    ✓ Thomas Jefferson ("Notes of a Tour through Holland and the Rhine Valley"; the languages he tried there were English, French, Italian, and Latin).

14. Why did John Quincy Adams regret not knowing Hebrew?

- ✓ He wanted to read the Bible in one of its original languages.

15. The controversial Fred Burks was an Indonesian interpreter for how many presidents?

    - ✓ Two (Bill Clinton and George W. Bush) Burks quit in 2004 because of government restrictions on his job. He would later reveal details of when he served as a presidential interpreter.

16. Which president often marked his books at the bottom with either a small T or a small I?

    - ✓ Thomas Jefferson (T was for Thomas, and I was the Latin form of J for Jefferson).

17. Which president's mahogany coffin had Latin inscriptions on it?

    - ✓ George Washington (two Latin inscriptions—"Surge Ad Judicium" (Rise to Judgment) and "Gloria Deo" (Glory to God))

18. What did John Quincy Adams cite as the reason he had trouble learning Italian?

    - ✓ Insufficient practice

19. Which president opined that French was "the international language of polite society?"

- ✓ George Washington thought it was useful to wealthy aristocrats, e.g., planters.

20. Which president was fond of the Russian phrase "doveryai no proveryai?"

    - ✓ Ronald Reagan (it means "trust but verify"; he used it in his dealings with the Soviets)

21. Which president wanted to learn German to travel to Berlin?

    - ✓ Woodrow Wilson (while he learned German, he never traveled to Berlin or even Germany)

22. The Latin phrase "Sic semper tyrannis" (thus [death] always to tyrants) is forever affiliated with which president?

    - ✓ Abraham Lincoln (it was shouted by his assassin, John Wilkes Booth)

23. Dwight Eisenhower spoke what language with a Kansan accident and with a Kansan vocabulary?

    - ✓ French (Eisenhower, from Kansas, took French at West Point and studied it daily while living in France)

24. Which president had a Spanish language home?

- ✓ Ronald Reagan ("Rancho del Cielo" (Ranch in the Clouds) was his California ranch.)

25. Which president said that "the flimsy prejudices of the French and English nations against the German language have long blinded them to the excellencies of its literature?"

    - ✓ John Quincy Adams (some thought him the father of German studies in America)

26. Who had a wife the French called the "La Belle Américaine" (the Beautiful American)?

    - ✓ James Monroe (his wife was Elizabeth Kortright)

27. Which president could not separate the French words, and although he could read it well and write it fairly well, he could not speak or understand it?

    - ✓ Dwight Eisenhower (he tried learning it in France during the 1920s)

28. Which president chose the Latin "Luxuria et egestas commodis cedun" (Wealth and power are inferior to what is comfortable) as the motto for his bookplate?

    - ✓ John Tyler (it reflected his disposition to seek moderation in all things).

29. What language did Zachary Taylor's interpreter speak?

    ✓ Seminole (his name was Abraham)

30. George Washington sent away to London for Latin books for which person?

    ✓ His stepson, Jackie Custis (these included a Latin-English dictionary and Latin grammars).

31. Which president critiqued a book about a universal language created by James Ruggles?

    ✓ John Quincy Adams (he gave it a tepid endorsement)

32. Which two presidents appeared in Germany's Christian Democratic Union political ads speaking German?

    ✓ John Kennedy and Bill Clinton (the ads quoted Kennedy's 1963 and Clinton's 1994 Berlin speeches)

33. Which president spoke French "without tense or gender" but was still easy to understand?

    ✓ Theodore Roosevelt (according to his Secretary of State John Hay).

34. Which president entertained people by writing simultaneously in Greek and Latin?

    ✓ James Garfield (he asked people questions and then answered them simultaneously in Greek and Latin)

35. Who vetoed his wife's attempt to force him to speak German at the dinner table?

    ✓ Woodrow Wilson (he gave it a try but gave up shortly thereafter; the purpose was to improve their children's German by hiring a German governess, Fraulein Clara Boehm).

36. Who stopped trying to speak French because "Everytime I tried to speak it, I'd make such a fool of myself"?

    ✓ Joe Biden (the same thing happened with Spanish except the Spanish would laugh with him)

37. Who called Greek "the most perfect instrument of thought"?

    ✓ James Garfield (he was a classics language professor at the Western Reserve Eclectic Institute (later Hiram College) in Ohio)

38. Of Dwight Eisenhower, his wife Mamie and son John, who had the best French?

    ✓ John (a student at a private American school in France, was much better in the language than his parents).

39. How many Latin expressions join George Washington on the one-dollar bill?

    ✓ Three ("annuit coeptis" - S/he approves of the undertakings; "novus ordo seclorum" - new order of the ages; and "e pluribus unum" —out of many, one).

ENGLISH IS A LANGUAGE TOO

1. What word did Donald Trump probably mean to say when he tweeted the words "negative press conference" in May 2017?

    ✓ "Coverage" (although Trump never confirmed this when asked for clarification)

2. Who said, "Do not expect me to run a country with a language as difficult as [English]?"

    ✓ Pope John XXIII facetiously dismissed concerns that the Catholic John Kennedy would take orders from him.

3. Who might have been the source for the English expression OK?

    ✓ Martin Van Buren (OK stands for "Old Kinderhook," meaning Van Buren, who was from Kinderhook, New York; source for OK is debated)

4. Which presidents had spouses whose first language was not English?

    ✓ Martin Van Buren (Dutch for Hannah Hoes, who died before he was president) and Donald Trump (Croatian for his current wife Melania and Czech for his first wife Ivana)

5. Which president's recommended spelling changes included "wisht" instead of "wished" and "caliber" instead of "calibre?"

    ✓ Theodore Roosevelt (in 1906, Congress blocked his attempt at simplified spelling).

6. Which English-language word did Warren G. Harding popularize?

    ✓ Bloviate (a verb meaning to speak pompously—he used it to describe his long-winded speaking style)

7. Who is erroneously credited with coining the English language term pussyfoot?

    ✓ Theodore Roosevelt (he used the term but did not invent it)

8. Who humorously claimed in a 2004 interview that "Bush's Spanish is better than his English"?

    ✓ NBC The Tonight Show host Jay Leno. His show poked fun at George W. Bush mispronouncing English words while showing him speaking Spanish with authority.

9. Which president said the following: "It is a damn poor mind that can think of only one way to spell a word?"

- ✓ Andrew Jackson (it was reflective of the time period—Benjamin Franklin once said that he "had no use for a man with but one spelling for a word.")

10. Who said the following: "Fluency in English is something that I'm often not accused of?"

    - ✓ George H.W. Bush (June 6, 1989, state dinner for Pakistani prime minister Benazir Bhutto)

11. Which president's failed spelling reforms included "embaras," "knolege," and "it's" (instead of "its")?

    - ✓ Thomas Jefferson (other failed reforms were not capitalizing Mr. and Mrs. nor the first word of the sentence).

12. Which president said the following: "The ten most dangerous words in the English language are 'Hi, I'm from the government, and I'm here to help'?"

    - ✓ Ronald Reagan (remarks to Future Farmers of America, July 28, 1988)

13. Which president supposedly pronounced cow with four syllables?

    - ✓ Calvin Coolidge (his wife Grace liked to imitate his nasal twang)

14. Which president popularized the term lunatic fringe?

    ✓ Theodore Roosevelt. ("a minority group of adherents to a political or other movement or set of beliefs") (the Oxford English Dictionary cites Roosevelt's 1913 quotation as the first usage).

15. To whom does Andrew Johnson credit with improving his writing skills?

    ✓ His wife, Eliza McCardle (she also read aloud to him; Johnson could barely read and could only spell a little).

16. Who caused a problem for interpreters with his statement, "When it comes to weapons systems, I am from Missouri?"

    ✓ Ronald Reagan. An interpreter had to know that Missouri's nickname is "the Show Me State, meaning Missourian's demand proof before believing. For Reagan, "seeing is believing."

17. Which president once called himself a verb rather than a personal pronoun?

    ✓ Ulysses Grant (On his 1885 deathbed, he told his doctor: I think I am a verb instead of a personal pronoun. A verb is anything that signifies to be to do, or to suffer. I signify all three.)

18. Which president popularized eracism (a movement to erase racism)?

    ✓ Bill Clinton (June 14, 1997 commencement address at the University of California, San Diego)

19. Which president coined the term "iffy" (describing a question, proposal, prospect, or decision that is full of ifs)?

    ✓ Franklin Delano Roosevelt warned in his first press conference that he would not answer "if" questions.

20. Which president popularized the term Snowmageddon?

    ✓ Barack Obama (February 8, 2010, Democratic National Committee meeting, in reference to the February 4, 2010 blizzard in Washington, DC, which shut down the federal government).

21. Which president was apparently the first to use "squatter" when referring to someone who occupies a property or territory he doesn't own?

- ✓ James Madison (1788 letter to George Washington complaining about Maine squatters)

22. Which president insisted on using the word "sugarcoat" (to coat with sugar and thus make palatable) despite being told it was inappropriate?

    - ✓ Abraham Lincoln (his message to Congress accused Southerners of having "sugarcoated" their rebellion)

23. Which president popularized "adams off ox" (not knowing the person at all)?

    - ✓ Bill Clinton (when asked about an Air Force official criticizing him, Clinton said, "And he doesn't know me from Adam's off ox." (June 15, 1993, press conference)

24. Which president redefined "caption" to mean "title" or "heading?"

    - ✓ James Madison ("You will see in the caption of the address that we have pruned the ordinary style of the degrading appendages of Excellency").

25. Which president coined the term "Michigander" for a native of Michigan?

- ✓ Abraham Lincoln (this was his derogatory term for Democratic Party presidential candidate Lewis Cass, who was from Michigan) "gander" is a male goose).

26. What was the term used to describe George W. Bush's English language adventures?

    - ✓ Bushisms (for example, he said, "They misunderestimated me." (November 6, 2000, Bentonville, Arkansas)

27. Which president popularized the golfing term "mulligan" (a "second chance" that is not counted on the scorecard.)?

    - ✓ Dwight Eisenhower (his "mulligan" was covered in the Washington Post May 18, 1947, sports section)

28. Using Pidgin English, which president asked his Pottawatomie tribe visitors, "Where live now?" and "When do you go back to Iowa?"

    - ✓ Abraham Lincoln (he also told them that the world was a great round ball)

29. Who mentioned Miss Julia Coleman in his inaugural address?

- ✓ Jimmy Carter (1977; he did not identify her as his English teacher).

30. How many times did Bill Clinton receive a Grammy for Best Spoken Word Album for Children?

    - ✓ Once (2004, for "Wolf Tracks and Peter and the Wolf"; He also won in 2005 for "My Life," but this was for Best Spoken Word Album only)

31. Who was reluctant to speak "foreign tongues" because the "purity of his English might be tainted"?

    - ✓ Woodrow Wilson (German was his foreign language of choice, however)

32. Who is the supposed source of the English word belittle?

    - ✓ Thomas Jefferson ("The Count de Buffon believes that nature belittles her productions on this side of the Atlantic.") (1788)

33. Who once wrote that "We have room for but one language here, and that is the English language, for we intend to see that the crucible turns our people out as Americans"?

    - ✓ Theodore Roosevelt (note to the American Defense Society, January 3, 1919)

34. Which president did not have English as a first language?

    ✓ Martin Van Buren (it was Dutch). Supposedly he was not fluent in English.

THOMAS JEFFERSON

1. Who doubted that Thomas Jefferson had learned Spanish in just nineteen days?

    ✓ John Quincy Adams (Jefferson told him in 1804 that he learned it during a transatlantic journey to France in 1784)

2. Thomas Jefferson never saw anyone speaking what three languages who did not mix them up.

    ✓ French, Spanish, and Italian (he called all three "degenerated dialects of Latin"; Italian in particular prevented mastery of the other two) (1787 letters to Peter Carr and T. M. Randolph Jr.)

3. Thomas Jefferson wanted to learn what language so that he could read Ossian's poems?

    ✓ Gaelic (1773 letter to Charles McPherson, who may have been the actual Ossian)

4. To whom did Thomas Jefferson give a large supply of blank vocabulary sheets?

    ✓ Lewis and Clark, who compiled word lists from Native American tribes while on their famous trek westward (1803-1806)

5. What language did Thomas Jefferson oppose teaching at the University of Virginia?

- ✓ Connecticut Latin (in 1825, he called it a "barbarous confusion of long and short syllables")

6. The last book that Thomas Jefferson read before dying was in what language?

    - ✓ Greek (according to his great-grandson, it was Aristotle's politics)

7. What language did Thomas Jefferson use in his 1825 version of The Lord's Prayer?

    - ✓ Anglo-Saxon ("Faeder ure thee the eart in heafenum," i.e., Our Father, which art in heaven.)

8. Which language did Thomas Jefferson think was "the least useful" for youth studying Latin, Greek, French and Spanish?

    - ✓ Greek (although he also said it was the most beautiful and finest of all languages (1819 letters to Mr. Moore and John Brazier, respectively)

9. According to Thomas Jefferson, what were the two most important foreign languages for Americans to learn?

    - ✓ French and Spanish (in that order) (he thought French for Americans was "indispensable").

10. What item was found within Thomas Jefferson's copy of Plutarch's Lives, Volume 2?

    ✓ A small scrap of Greek writing

11. What misfortune affected Thomas Jefferson's collection of Native American vocabularies?

    ✓ A trunk containing more than 40 Native American vocabularies disappeared in transit between Washington, DC, and his Monticello home.

12. According to Thomas Jefferson, what Native American language proved that all words were not originally monosyllabic as believed?

    ✓ Cherokee, which used phrases rather than single words, proving his viewpoint.

www.ingramcontent.com/pod-product-compliance
Lightning Source LLC
Chambersburg PA
CBHW052034030426
42337CB00027B/4996